Angela L. Washington
3839 E 154th St.
Cleveland, OH 44128
216-258-5647
iahosen57@yahoo.com

MY JOURNEY TO THE OTHER SIDE OF THROUGH

BY ANGELA L. WASHINGTON

This book is a memoir. It reflects the author's present recollections of experiences over time. Some events have been compressed, and some dialogue has been recreated.

ISBN: **979-8-8689-5535-8**

DEDICATIONS

This book is dedicated to all the broken-hearted. To those that are on their journey to the other side of through. Without God none of this would be possible. I also would like to thank Mr. Jerome Washington. My children Antoine, April, and Aaron. My grandchildren Syncere and DJ. My Aunts Paulette and Eloise. Thank you for supporting my dream.

MY JOURNEY TO THE OTHER SIDE OF THROUGH

Table of Contents

ACKNOWLEDGMENTS

I would like to thank my heavenly father for giving me the creativity to write my journey.

My church family has been such an inspiration, helping me keep hope alive. Every time I was discouraged, they gave me strength to stay in the race and not to give up. Especially our prayer line. What an awesome group of people. They all have the same goal in mind. That goal is to uplift, encourage, and love those that are in need of prayer.

Special thanks Lisa Finley by bestie for life. To my work daughters Victoria, Melony, Latura, Caitlyn, Julie, and Taje. I am so proud that you guys consider me to be an inspiration in your lives. Thanks, and shout-out to Ms. Tammy Johnson, my publisher. I appreciate your guidance, patience, and generosity in making my vision become reality.

INTRODUCTION

My name is Angela L. Washington, and this book is about my life's journey and how I persevered to reach the other side of my destiny.

This book entails my journey from childhood until my current and present moment. You will find that I was a girl with many obstacles and challenges. Obstacles and challenges that should have destroyed my very existence. However, I learned how to Push- Pray Until Something Happens.

My prayer is reading this book; will help those who are struggling find their purpose. Keep reaching, striving, and stay the course until you find your other side of through.

Chapter 1

And She Shall Be Called Angela

It was a cold spring day the year I was born 1964. You would think being born at the end of April springtime would be in the air. That was not the case with my birth. In fact, it was quite the opposite. My mom was a pregnant teen. She got pregnant with my sister at the age of fourteen. My sister was born when my mom turned fifteen years old. Since she was so young, my grandmother and grandfather took care of my older sister. However, when my mom met my dad, she became pregnant again. My grandfather told my dad he should marry my mother. He said he wasn't going to be responsible for another child coming into their home. So, my parents were forced to marry. My dad did not like that option, but it was the hand he was dealt. At this time, my mother was turning sixteen years old. There it was, me being born when she was sixteen. My dad was in his early twenties. At first, there were speculations regarding my birth. One of my father's aunts didn't believe I was my dad's daughter.

Unfortunately, my mom was promiscuous. Doubts entered the mindset of family members, especially my aunt Ethel. Aunt Ethel had a discerning character. She said she could feel when something wasn't right. In her mind, this situation didn't rest well with her. She tried to convince my dad he would be making a mistake and to reconsider the marriage. This went on a couple of months before my parents were married.

Since my mom really loved my dad, she wanted to prove my aunt wrong. She prayed and asked God to let me look like my dad or someone on that side of the family. Sure enough, I came out looking like my dad. Genetics played a factor in my appearance. I had sandy hair, a wide nose, and fair complexion. My complexion was definitely my mother's. Everything else was my dad's. The proof was definitely in the pudding.

My grandparents welcomed me with open arms. They were happy that my parents were taking care of me instead of them. As we delve into further chapters, you will see how this family dynamic will change. My parents had a difficult time with choosing a name for me. Names were thrown out but none of them seemed to fit. My grandmother said I should be named Angela. This did not sit well with my dad because he wanted to name me Tina Marie.

He had finally come up with a name for me, but my grandma stole his thunder. Looking back, I would have been named after an R&B singer. My grandmother knew there would be something special in naming me Angela. My name means messenger of God. Later we'll see how my name fits my destiny.

Our neighbor's daughter shared her middle name with me. Her middle name was Lanelle. I was born Angela Lanelle Davis on April 27, 1964. I was blessed to have so many aunts and uncles. My dad came from a large family. He was the eldest of sixteen children. There were originally eighteen but two passed away. That left the sixteen. My dad's side of the family had a strong spiritual background. My dad's parents instilled the Pentecostal faith in all of their children. My dad and all of his siblings had spiritual gifts beyond measure, mostly in the gospel music arena. These gifts would pass on throughout our generation.

Being born second came with perks and privileges. Since I was the baby at that moment, I got spoiled rotten. Of course, I did. Isn't that what happens when you are the baby? Everyone wants to do for you because you're so cute, loveable, and adorable. Well at least that's what I thought.

Chapter 2

Childhood Memories

My childhood was filled with good and bad memories. First, I'll talk about the good, then we will get to the bad. As previously stated, I was reaping the benefits of being the baby. My mom treated me like a princess. Having nice clothes was never a second thought. She made sure I was dressed from head to toe. Every outfit I wore had matching socks and shoes. I learned how to be a little diva early thanks to my mom.

Whatever I wanted I got. I remember wanting a puppy. I desired to have an all-black dog because I wanted to name him Blackie. Would you believe I got him along with a cat and a bird? I was the luckiest little girl in the world. Three pets for the price of one. Talk about the pampered life. I was in heaven.

In my eyesight, my father and my mother were my heroes. My mom worked at the Board of Education. She had a great job and a great salary. My Dad worked at Howard Johnson's, a well-known restaurant in the Cleveland area. He was a great chef. My dad could make the best barbecue. My mother was classy. She dressed in fur, beautiful jewelry, and was just well put together. She always had an eye for fashion and nice things. Even my mom's co-workers treated me well. Sometimes she would take me to work with her. She had a friend name Nina who was from Germany.

Nina introduced me to German culture. She would bring schnitzel and sauerkraut to work. It was different yet I liked it.

Growing up in the African American culture you are accustomed to eating, greens, cornbread, and fried chicken. To say the least, Nina sparked my interest in another culture other than my own. Someday I would love to go to Germany. Nina talked about Berlin and Hamburg often. Her city was on the borders of Hamburg and Berlin. Yes, life was good until that terrible day happened.

My Dad and Mom were growing apart. Tension was in the air with lots of arguing. I didn't understand what was happening. At this time, my dad began drinking. He was a full-blown alcoholic. If you have never been around an alcoholic, you can't possibly understand the challenges it brings. While my mom was at work, my dad would bring his women around me. I thought they were his co-workers or friends of his and my mom's; they weren't. I don't know how my mom found out, but she did. She was devastated. Just when we had the perfect family, my dad ruined it with his women and drinking. My mom was given no other option but to get a divorce. This cut like a knife. Needless to say, I hated this moment of my life.

At this point, my father was hostile. He kidnapped me at gunpoint. He didn't want a divorce and thought this would stop my mother, but it didn't. I was so afraid. Why would my daddy do this? After the final decree was made, my parents moved on with their lives. I wanted them back together, but it did not happen. I had so many questions rambling in my head. I cried for days. I blamed my dad for the deterioration of my family dynamic.

To my surprise, I didn't think I would like my new stepdad. My mom had remarried and so did my dad. My stepdad was a nice southern gentleman. Since I acquired a taste for food, I fell in love with his cooking. My dad on the other hand married a recovering addict. It seems they were made for each other. She had a daughter. He treated them better than he treated me. How dare he? I was his only child but got treated as the stepdaughter. I felt like an outcast. My mom loved me but not enough to make me and my sister part of her new world. My mom said and I quote, " Do you want to come with me or what?" She was moving to Chicago with her new husband. You don't ask your young child that question. You're the parent. Once again, I was left confused and bewildered, especially since she left me with my grandmother. This was the beginning of my abandonment and mistrust issues.

I felt betrayed by the people who were supposed to love and protect me. I thought this must be a mistake. She was just kidding, right? However, this was not a fairy tale or dream. Reality was setting in and I could not cope. Every day I looked for my parents thinking they were coming to get me. Weeks turned into months and months turned into years. My heart was so broken from their actions. How could both of them leave me behind? It seems as if they have no remorse for the choices they've made. I did not want to live with my grandmother. She wasn't my mom or Dad. I had a hard time adjusting to what was about to be my new normal. I thought to myself this totally sucks.

Chapter 3

From Princess to Ordinary Jane

Living with my grandmother was very challenging. My grandmother was around 50 when she took me in. My older sister was already there. During this time, my grandfather had passed. He was my Mom's Dad. This left my grandmother a widow with two young girls. She depended on him for everything. Life for me had changed drastically.

My life of being pampered was no longer a factor. Pretty clothes and shoes were out of the question. My grandmother couldn't afford such luxuries for me. I went from being a princess to plain Jane. The whole atmosphere was so chaotic. Sometimes I wish I had never had parents. I wouldn't be going through hell and turmoil of this new life.

Growing up in the house with my grandmother taught me how to stand on my feet. She was a wise old woman. I thank God for that. Despite her verbal abuse, she instilled value in my sister and me. We were taught the basic necessities of survival.

She was a single woman raising two abandoned girls. We were taught how to cook early in life. Back then it was the norm for young girls to learn cooking and sewing. We were taught the overall duties of being a young lady. Again, my grandmother showed us these things. On the flip side, she was very abusive. There were so many times I got the brunt of my grandmother's anger.

As I began to get older, my behavior was beginning to look like my mom's all over again. I remember being around nine or ten years old and my grandmother asked me a question. She said, "Do you think you are better than me and your sister?" I politely said yes. That's when she hit me in the mouth and told me not to sass her. I didn't feel like I was doing that. I just believed I was better because of the lifestyle I had with my parents.

Don't get me wrong, I knew my grandmother was struggling since my grandad passed away. She was dealing with unresolved grief. Her emotions showed up in her abuse towards me. My ego was destroyed by her abusive words. Jesus loves the little children was my favorite biblical song. I asked myself if Jesus loves the little children why didn't he love me? Why did he allow such verbal abuse against me? Here comes issue number three, anger. I was angry with God, angry because my mom and dad were divorced, angry at my grandmother's verbal abuse, and angry at my current lifestyle. I had become an angry little bird. My grandmother did the best she could by providing for me and my sister. We were on public assistance. It was not enough to take care of us. My grandmother got a job at the local supermarket. She was a meat cutter. Whenever we came home from school, meals were prepared. Since we did not have a microwave, we warmed the food on top of the stove or the oven.

With her working long hours, she was away from us a lot. She needed a babysitter to watch us. Our neighbor had a teenage daughter. My grandmother paid for her neighbor's daughter to babysit us. Things were okay until our babysitter started showing odd behavior. She always wanted me to be close to her. I knew this was strange. Being a kid, I thought it was kind of okay. It was not. I had become a victim of molestation.

I was too scared to tell my grandmother because she was good friends with the neighbor. My grandmother wouldn't have believed me anyway. She saw me as my mother. The shame I carried around was painful. Well, God removed her because she moved to another state. She wouldn't have the opportunity to continue the abuse. Something broke in me during this time. I felt I couldn't trust anyone. Insecurities, fear, and mistrust was my name. I began to act out because of this. My grandmother had no idea what was going on. She saw me as a disrespectful child and chastised me. Chastising me only made matters worse as it related to my behavior.

Chapter 4

Teenage Blues

Okay, so now I am at the age of twelve. Puberty had settled in. My body was beginning to develop. Every summer my grandmother sent my sister and me to my mom's. As previously stated, my mother was living in Chicago. My grandmother felt my mother needed to be responsible for us. Since she had us most of the time, she felt my mother should have us in the summer. By this time, my mother had my younger brother and was pregnant with my little sister.

It was a treat when my grandmother would send me there. I got to spend time with my family. It was 1976 and a hot summer in Chicago. My stepdad, mother, and little brother lived in a studio apartment. The space was crowded but it was durable. This particular day my mother asked me to clear the cabinets for the exterminator. Of course, I wasn't thrilled about doing that.

I told my mom that grandma doesn't make me do things like that. My mom said she didn't care that was her house and I will do what she says. So, I did it. My brother was acting mischievous like a typical kid. I don't know the extent of what he did. Whatever it was he got reprimanded for it.

I didn't realize my brother had loose membranes in his nostrils. They caused nosebleeds. When I saw my brother's nose bleeding, I thought my mom was the cause of it. Although, she wasn't. I asked my mom why she did that. Again, there's that angry little bird coming out. She asked me what I said. I reared up at her with a stern voice and said why did you hit him? I'm going to tell your mama. She said are you talking back to me. I said yes and you better not hit him again.

The fight was on. She pushed. I pushed back. She hit me. I hit back. You would have thought we were Ali and Frazier. The final blow came when she knocked me under the kitchen table. At this point, I realized what respect was. Even though she wasn't raising me, she was still my mother. Over and over again I tried to forget this moment. The next summer when I went back. I treated my mom with a little more respect. When you lose respect for someone, it is hard to give. Especially if it is a parent who has abandoned you. My stepdad decided he wanted to go to Mississippi. That is where he was born. My sister had left a couple of months early. My stepdad, mom, little brother, and I were headed to Mississippi. Talking about a long drive, it took fourteen or sixteen hours to get there.

I enjoyed sightseeing. I had never seen the Mississippi River. Watching the River Boats with the steam rollers was impressive. Experiencing Southern hospitality was different from the North. The fried chicken was crisper, and the cakes were mouth-watering. My stepdad's mom lived around the corner from Walter Payton. Payton had just won the Heisman Trophy.

They had the trophy in the window where everyone could see it. It was huge, gold, and shiny. With Payton winning the Heisman Trophy, it jump started his career. Payton signed with the Chicago Bears. I don't know football statistics, but Payton had a rushing game out of this world. God Bless you Walter you will forever be in our hearts.

Since I was in the North, I wasn't familiar with racism. It was a hot night and my cousins, and I decided to go for a stroll. The air was crisp and invigorating. We began to walk down a little dirt road. From out of nowhere, a truck appeared. In the truck were three white males. One of them yelled out and said" where do you niggers think you're going. I was about to say something to them. One of my cousins pinched me so hard it brought tears to my eyes.

After they left, I asked why she pinched me that way. She told me she was protecting me. I said from what. She said they could have raped us. This was a cultural shock for me. At least we had a little more freedom up North. I was learning a lot this particular summer. I remember going to the bathroom and blood gushed out of me. Just like the movie Carrie, I started my cycle and was scared to death. I screamed and hollered until my cousin came into the bathroom. She laughed at me. I didn't think it was funny. She said now you are approaching womanhood. I told her I didn't want any part of this because it was nasty. Being uninformed made me realize how important it was to have a mother. My grandma was old and probably didn't know how to approach the subject matter. I got cleaned up and was ready for the next time it happened. I was very well developed at twelve. I looked sixteen.

I met a boy at the local market. He thought I was older and wanted to take me for ice cream. I let him. I wasn't going to tell him I was only twelve. We got ice cream and then the unmentionable happened. He French kissed me. I asked why he did that. He said he did that to all the pretty girls. Of course, I was flattered. However, I was only twelve years old and wasn't ready for that. I guess that's what I get for lying about my age. The summer ended and I was prepared to go back to Cleveland. My stepdad dropped a bomb on me. Here I was thinking this was just a summer vacation. However, it was not. He didn't return to Chicago. I was stuck in Mississippi. It was a month before school started. I cried. I didn't want to live in the South. I felt an unease, especially after my encounter with racism. My great-grandparents were living at the time. They got wind of what happened. Next thing you know I was on a bus back to Cleveland.

Excitement was in the air. I didn't have to stay in Mississippi after all. I would go to school on time and be with my friends. I was so thankful for my great-grandparents. They had compassion for me. They made sure that I wouldn't miss school.

Chapter 5

School Daze

Returning back to school was awesome. I was in my first year of Junior High. In those days, you graduated out of sixth grade going to seventh through ninth grade. Then from tenth grade until twelfth grade. Seventh grade was fun. I had developed friends who were funny and free-spirited like me. I love hanging around them. Although I attended an all-girl school, boys still hung around. I was the nerdy type. I wasn't really interested in boys. I was all about the books.

I loved school. Science was my favorite subject. I was fascinated learning about organisms and how they are formed. I also like Social Studies. Everyone should know about history. History is what makes the world go around. These were my two favorite subjects. Math on the other hand was not.

For some reason, looking at numbers and trying to calculate them was annoying. I was getting through it by the hairs of my chinney chin chin. It was my least favorite subject. Home economics was another class I loved. They need to bring these types of classes back. Young girls today don't get taught some of these basic necessities. These classes prepare you for family and independent living. I was happy to take them. I realized that someday I may have a family. Cooking and sewing classes were necessary. Although my grandmother had prepared me, the extra course study kicked me into high gear.

Since Junior High went from seventh to ninth grade, one of my friends was a ninth grader. We had teacher student day back then. All ninth graders who were graduating would become teachers for the day. Becoming teacher of the day, the student had to have at least a 3.0 average, and a good attendance record. My friend Bridget had all the above. My math teacher was named Mr. Zuckerman. Bridget met the requirements for becoming teacher of the day. Our math teacher, Mr. Zuckerman, gave Bridget the chart plan to follow. She was thrilled that she was chosen to be the teacher. This meant that Mr. Zuckerman would portray the student. At first glance, this was a fun day. Bridget did a great job with being our math instructor. Mr. Zuckerman on the other hand would find out that being the student for the day was not in his best interest. Again, I struggled with Math. While Bridget was assigning the group math project, Mr. Zuckerman found the need to distract me. He would constantly throw paper at me. Until this day, I never understood why he did that. Anyway, as politely as I could I asked him not to throw paper at me.

He didn't listen. Mind you I am going on thirteen years old. That little bird was being contained but he was about to bring it out again. I gave him an ultimatum. I told him if he threw one more piece of paper at me, I was going to hit him in the mouth. Like that old saying goes "You think fat meat ain't greasy". Well, he was about to find out. I allowed him to slide. He threw another piece of paper at me. By this time, I am really angry. I gave him one more chance. He threw that last piece, and it gave me a paper cut. Class had ended. There is always an instigator around. One of my classmates said Angela you're not going to hit him in his mouth. I said oh really and did just that. They called my grandma. I said Angela you are in big trouble now.

Grandma came to school and had a conference with Mr. Zuckerman. I thought I would get suspended. To my surprise I wasn't even reprimanded. My grandmother told him about the errors of his ways.

Despite him being the student for the day, he was still an adult and had a responsibility to me and the rest of the class. He shouldn't be throwing paper or anything at me. I felt so proud of my grandma for standing up for me.

This was the first time she ever believed me about anything. I graduated from Junior High and went to high school. High School was definitely not Junior High. I was not a little girl anymore but a young lady. I was still nerdy, but I found myself liking boys. They would say I was cute. I would fall for it every time. When I was in tenth grade, I went to John Hay High school. Since I loved the sciences, taking chemistry was right up my alley. At the time Charles Oakley was in my chemistry class. He would later become a professional basketball player. I remember working on a chemistry project with him. It was a fun time. When he got drafted by the Cavaliers, we were so happy for him. He was a kid from our city and high school. I spent one year at John Hay.

During my junior and senior year, I was bussed to Glenville. They began bussing students who lived in a particular geographical zone. According to where I lived, I got bussed. Just when I was getting familiar with making friends, I had to change schools. While I was in the eleventh grade, I took a business work study program. There I learned secretarial skills. I mastered the art of typing with proficiency and accuracy. My business teacher took notice. She saw that I was the fastest typist in the class. I made minimum mistakes when typing up projects. She felt that I had leadership potential.

We developed a special club within our business work study program. I was nominated as the secretary. Along with the nomination for the position, I had the privilege of being inducted into the National Honor Society. I never thought this would happen to me. Well, someone was interested in me. My friend introduced me to who would be my boyfriend. He was two years older than me. We started out well, but things got a little rocky. However, we managed to stay together.

Fast forwarding now to my senior year. Life as a senior was challenging. I realized that adult life was about to happen. Keeping my grades up, selecting colleges, and being in a serious relationship was my focus. Trying to balance this felt overwhelming. I managed because I was determined not to let anything get in my way. Well, something did get in the way. I went to the emergency room. I kept having bad stomach pain. They said I had gastritis. Well, another doctor ran some tests. It wasn't gastritis. I was pregnant.

I was in disbelief. I tried to be careful with protection, but I guess I wasn't.

Chapter 6

Relationships 101 X 101

Here I am a senior and pregnant. What would I do with a baby? How was I going to explain this to my grandmother? Better yet how would I tell him he was going to be a dad? All I could think about was prom and graduation. I would have to attend both of them with a belly. My grades began to slip. I yet persevered.

Just like before, I went to the bathroom and blood began to gush out. This time I wasn't twelve, having my first cycle. I was eighteen and had a miscarriage. I lost my baby in the toilet. I was devastated and relieved at the same time. The Lord knew I wasn't ready to have a baby. Yes, it was unfortunate. Emotionally, and mentally the whole thought of having a baby stressed me out. I was glad I didn't have to worry about it anymore. There was no need to tell him or my grandmother what happened. I blocked it from my mind. I was able to go to the prom and graduate.

I remember I couldn't afford a beautiful prom dress like all the other girls in my senior class. One of my best friends was in a wedding. I told her that I didn't have a dress to wear. I was going to get my dress from the thrift store. Well, since she was my best friend, she let me borrow her dress she wore in the wedding. It was a pretty baby blue and ivory. She let me borrow another outfit for the after prom. I was back to being a princess. That's what I call a true friend.

It was two weeks before graduation and they posted the class rankings. After my miscarriage, I worked diligently to get my grades back up. I had fallen to a 2.5 but got it back up to a 3.0 average. When I saw the rankings, I was in the upper 20 percent of the class. I was number 9. Tears of joy flooded my eyes. I would graduate. My Mom and Dad attended my graduation but to me it wasn't a big deal. I was happy they were there, but I could take it or leave it. My Granny was there to support me.

I had won the Presidential Scholarship to Dyke Business College. I had a full scholarship. College life was going great. One day I called my boyfriend's mom to speak with him. She said he wasn't home. I asked what time he was coming back. She hesitated, and said he wasn't he moved out of state. Did I just get dumped by this man? Just when I was healing from my abandonment issues, he re-created them. Why does this keep happening? Everyone I seem to love keeps leaving me. I felt that I could not live without him. So, I got on a greyhound bus and followed him to California. When I got there, I thought he would take me to a nice apartment. I was in shock. He lived in a motel. That's where we were going to live. What did I get myself into? I gave up my education just to be with him. Living with him was great despite where we lived. We did our best to make it a home until the toxicity took place. He was physically abusive. I tried to overlook his behavior, but it was impossible.

One night while he was at work, I went across the street to the church in our neighborhood. I asked God to give me a son. For some reason I was feeling remorse for the baby I had lost. I wanted someone to love me and for me to love them back. He came home and I remember having the biggest smile on my face.

He asked me what had me smiling. I told him in time he would see. Little did he know what I asked God for. I believed that one day the Lord would answer my prayer. I so wanted to be loved. I knew if I had a child my child would love me, and I would love him. Although I didn't realize you could speak life in existence. I trusted God for my miracle.

<u>Chapter 7</u>

California Living

Living in California was truly an eye opener. Ohio was not a state that openly displayed the LGBTQ community. It was the early 80's and the LGBTQ community was alive and well in San Francisco. I was totally clueless as it related to queer lifestyle. We had a transgender in our motel. I thought she was a female. However, she was a male. I learned that no matter what your gender is you are still a human being. She would become one of my closet friends in the building.

My boyfriend decided that it would be best if we separated. We both joined an organization called the California

Conservation Corps. The Corps was an excellent way to jump start a trade. They taught you how to preserve the environment. We did sand bagging for floods and disasters, how to fight forest fires, and brick laying. Since I loved to cook. They sent me to culinary school. I became a supervising cook at the age of 19. He and I would meet up every three months.

One day I was cooking and passed out. I was rushed to the infirmary. Would you believe God answered my prayer? I was pregnant and he was a boy. I would have someone to love me. Things were going well until I found out that he betrayed me. He had a relationship with my best friend.

I left California and moved to Chicago with my family. My son was born in Chicago. I gave him everything. My mom helped me take care of him. My younger brother and sister were great babysitters. They were young themselves, but they always helped their big sister out. However, the roles were reversed. My mom began partying again. She and my stepdad were divorced. She had taken up with a gentleman that was not good for her. I became a mother to my son and my younger siblings. I found myself being the mom and the big sister at the same time.

I did not like my mother's companion. He worked but he was irresponsible. Making money is fine. However, when you waste it and don't use it wisely it isn't fine. That is what he did. He wasted his money on alcohol and drugs. People would be in and out of my mom's apartment all the time. There was an incident where alcohol spilled onto my son's bottle. That was the day I popped off. I was 20 years old, and I loved being a mom. I wasn't going to let anything, or anyone harm me, my baby, or my siblings. I was not living a Christian life, so my words were very choice if you know what I mean. By the time I read him his rights, and I do mean he got read well; he didn't do that again.

I found work in downtown Chicago. It was a non-profit organization. It paid part-time because I was receiving government assistance. I met a man that was fifteen years older than me. He was 35.

He took good care of me. He took me to fancy restaurants, bought me expensive clothes, and arranged for me to have a babysitter. He knew how difficult it was in the house for me. Finally, I had a stable relationship. My son and I were doing great. However, he was somewhat controlling. I remember he wanted me to move in with him. I thought about it, but something kept nudging me not to do it. I was glad I didn't. Again, he was too controlling.

He wanted me to dress a certain way. He didn't want me to hang out with my friends or go anywhere without him. That definitely was not going to happen. So, I ended the relationship. To my surprise I received a letter from my ex. He stated how sorry he was and that he wanted to be a family. I thought maybe I should give him another chance to redeem himself.

Chapter 8

Reconnecting

I was re-connecting with him. Things were going well so I decided to give him another chance. So back to California I went. My son was 1 year old at the time. I felt he really wanted to be a family. He picked up us from the airport. He looked like he had matured. When we got into the apartment, it was beautiful. It was a townhome. Much nicer than the motel. I was so happy. However, I noticed there was a young lady there. I knew he was in a relationship, and he told me she was moving out. I respected that.

She had a daughter, and they were to move the week after I came. The next week came, and they were still there. Then the next week after that. He said he wanted to tell me his plan in person. I said what plan. He said he wanted us to be a family. Not just me and our son, but her daughter and herself as well. I was livid. I had a one-way ticket and couldn't afford to go back to Chicago. Idiot was written on my forehead. I fell for it again. Living in the apartment was like the Cinderella story. I was the caretaker. I washed, cleaned, took care of the kids, and cooked.

My son and I slept on the floor. They had bedrooms. So many nights I cried and realized the terrible mistake I made. I put our son in a compromising position. I started going to school so I couldn't care for the children anymore. They found a reliable babysitter for her daughter and our son. One day while I was taking them to the babysitter's, I met a young man. He was impressed with my son's outfit. He was wearing a little pair of 501 jeans by Levi Strauss. I dressed our son the way my mom used to dress me.

We exchanged numbers and went out on a couple of dates. At this point, I didn't care about his father. He made his choice by choosing her. I developed a relationship with him, but it wasn't romantic. We were just great friends. We hung out all the time. One night an intimate moment happened. It wasn't that we wanted it to. It just happened. We still remain friends. That didn't destroy our friendship.

It was a Tuesday, and my son's father told me that he had an out-of-town guest coming. I asked who it was, and he told me it wasn't my concern and our son, and I had to leave. I said, "Where would I go?" and he said he didn't know and didn't care. We had just become homeless. He kicked us out. Here I was in another state with no family or job. My son and I lived in a homeless shelter for a couple of months.

What had I done to deserve this cruel treatment? I tried to make the best of the situation. I had to constantly protect my son and me from the other people at the shelter. I hid food so my baby would have something to eat. Even if I didn't eat, I made sure he would. I was so hurt. I didn't want this lifestyle for me and my son, but I was left with no option. A group of church women would hold services at the shelter. I remember a church mother. Her name was Mother Alexander and she had six sons. All six of her sons were in the church. I didn't understand the Pentecostal faith, but I knew it was what my grandparents taught.

Out of everyone in the shelter, Mother Alexander had a special place in her heart for me and my son. She would always bring us extra items. These items consisted of food, blankets, diapers, and hygiene products.

One day, Mother Alexander asked me was I tired of living in the shelter. I told her yes. However, the cards were stacked against me. She then asked if I wanted to live with her and the boys. I was glad to oblige. God had smiled on me. We lived with Mother Alexander until I could get back on my feet. I applied for benefits from the county. They came through. I was able to get housing for me and my son. This allowed me to become independent. I had my baby, and we were fine. I realized I didn't have to settle or go back to the place where I didn't want.

My neighbors were Mexican. Sometimes they would watch my son while I was job hunting. I met a young lady named Matar. We were applying for the same job. We hit it off immediately. She became a dear friend. She had gotten the job instead of me. She always looked out for me. I had an interview for another job. I needed my hair done but couldn't afford to go the salon. Matar, washed, conditioned, and styled my hair so I would look nice for the interview. I was able to work 20 hours and still receive my benefits.

Our mail ran on Wednesdays. I went to the mailbox to get my check, but it wasn't there. I thought to myself, perhaps the mail was slow. I looked for it the next day. It still wasn't there. Matar had extra keys to my house. I trusted her. However, I found out otherwise. My neighbors never liked Matar. They told me they overheard her plotting how she was going to take my mail which included my check.

Here we go again. Hurt, mistrust, and betrayal was still holding on to me like bees to a honeycomb. Matar had me set-up. I thought I had found a reliable friend. She wasn't. Something must have been wrong with me. Why did I keep allowing these people in my life? Was I that gullible?

Chapter 9

Familiar Territory

I called the county and told them what happened. They asked me did if I wanted to prosecute Matar. I told them no. One thing I remembered my grandmother telling me is this," Don't try to get even with people because God is the ultimate justifier. Karma would take place." Well, it did, she stole from someone else and ended up in prison. I quit the job I had. The county replaced my benefits along with my check. Once I received them, I made up my mind to go back to familiar territory. I went back home to Cleveland. I spent the last four years in California. I was 22 years old at the time.

I called my grandmother, and she said yes, I could come home. She knew I had my son, but I also would be coming home with someone else. I was pregnant again with baby number two. My grandmother had changed somewhat. Her words were not as abusive. I had my daughter and we lived under the same roof with her and my sister. I wanted more for me and my children. I re-enrolled back into Dyke Business College.

I wanted an education. I wanted a career to support me and my kids. I was working toward obtaining my associate degree. It would be in Office Management Systems. One morning, as I was on my way to school, I saw a handsome young man on the bus. I catch this bus every day. I never paid attention to him, but on this day I did. He was drop dead gorgeous. He was dressed professionally, and I was impressed with his whole appearance. He even had a monogrammed briefcase and that really got my attention.

We talked on the phone for hours and hours. I really enjoyed speaking with him. We went on a date, and we had so much fun. Unfortunately, we lost contact with each other. I really missed him. I didn't see him on the bus anymore. I remember being in the discount drug Mart and when I looked down the aisle it was him. I was as happy as a kid receiving a toy at Christmas.

He was still dropped dead gorgeous. I asked if he remembered me. (I was hoping he would) he said yes but he forgot my name. I thought to myself, how could he forget my name? I felt some kind of way. We began to go on a lot of dates. I had my own apartment. I started cooking for him. We were comfortable with each other. I gave myself to him because he made me feel safe.

My children were staying between my apartment and my grandmother's house. He and I went to my neighbor's hotel party. What a great time we had. Every time I would dance, I would feel a sharp pain in my side. I was like I know I don't have arthritis. I was only 25 years old. I was pretty healthy. I didn't think anything of it. We came back to my apartment and fell asleep in each other's arms.

The next day I woke up and it was still happening. I was getting sharp pains in my joints and sides. He said he was taking me to the urgent care. When we arrived, they asked me the routine questions. Did I have a fever? How long was the pain? How many days did it happen? I answered them. They felt the need to give me a urine test. They were trying to see if I had a bladder infection. At first, it looked like it. My urine had a trace of blood in it. It was just a small amount. They still said they needed to do one more test. He and I are getting nervous now.

I asked him what he thought this was. He said he had no idea. They came back and said, Ms. Davis, you are pregnant. I was so happy because I wanted to have his baby. We looked at each other. He said hello mommy and I said hello daddy. We were overjoyed.

Chapter 10

On the Other side of through

I was about to be a mom of three and loving it. We eventually got married and started our family. There were many days challenges came. However, like most parents we were faced with some difficulty at it related to our children. When the children were smaller, we lived in East Cleveland. We had bought a house on a street called Nelaview. It was a friendly little street. Everyone there was family oriented. During this time, my oldest was going to high school, and my daughter and baby were in junior high and elementary school.

My son's prom was the highlight of the street. The year was 2002. He had a black stretch limousine. I felt it would be safer for him if someone else was doing the driving. Although he had a license, it was better that way. His date was so adorable. She stood at 4'11 inches. He graduated and moved to Atlanta, Georgia. He got accepted at Clark Atlanta University. He was a pre-med major and carried a 4.0. grade average. I was so proud of him. Two years later his sister went to prom, and when she graduated, she moved to California. This was hard for me. I developed Separation Anxiety. My babies had been with me all their lives. I couldn't cope with them leaving me. Again, I was never over my abandonment issues. I had my baby boy and husband, so I adapted. They both were thriving as adults until one day I got a phone call from my son. His tone had changed, and he was acting somewhat strangely. Next thing you know, he was coming back to Cleveland. His behavior was stranger by the minute. Too make a long story short my son was suffering from a mental illness. How could this be from someone who had the brain of Einstein?

Previously, I had lost my grandmother and it affected him tremendously. The matriarch was gone. I tried not to beat myself up, but I couldn't comprehend what a mental illness was. I never was around anyone who had that type of disorder. I took him to a therapist, and he received medicine. There were days when he was low and days when he was demonstrating manic behavior. I stuck by him through thick and thin. We started losing family members in 2001. It seemed like every year we were losing more and more of our close loved ones. Death had taken its toll on our family. From 2001 until now we have lost loved ones. An average person would not be able to cope. I thank God for strong faith.

In 2010, my life got turned upside down. I was at work and received a phone call from Metro hospital. The person on the other end said there was a car accident my oldest son was involved in. They said they would need to do emergency surgery. I went into panic mode. When I got there, my son was in a coma. Here he was on life support. Five weeks before this, I lost my uncle who was on life support as well. This was like déjà vu. I couldn't lose my child. This was when the Lord spoke to me and asked me who He was. I said you are God. God answered me and said, "I will restore him."

The doctors told me he would be a vegetable because he was tossed with his brain outside of his skull. They said there was nothing else they could do. I remember what God said. I stayed at the hospital day and night. One Sunday at church, a minister said call out what you want the Lord to do. I said I want my son to be able to eat, walk, and talk. Since my son was in a coma, he couldn't do any of those things. I got to the hospital. I had an urgency to call his sister.

She was still living in California. I say I am going to put the phone up to your brother's ear.

She said he cannot talk or understand me. He is in a coma. I said start talking. She spoke to him and said the same thing twice, "Brother, I love you." On the third time he called out his sister's name. Her name is April. I flew through the wings of the hospital proclaiming what God had done. God is never slack on his promises.

My son went to rehab and started walking, talking, and eating. What a miracle and testimony. That was in 2010. In 2014, I went to work and didn't feel well that day. In previous years I was diagnosed as a diabetic. My numbers were a little high that day but not too alarming. I punched in on the computer and fell backwards. I had a massive stroke. The stroke team came and took me to the ER. They gave me a TPA to stop the clot from traveling. I was life-flighted and placed on the Neuro Surgical Intensive Care fighting for my life.

Conclusion

Once again, God proved himself to me. He will never leave you or forsake you. I found this out. All the time I tried to run from Him, he made me run to Him. I recognized what truth faith was. I had to find out God's power for me. I always knew I had a calling on my life. This was the real proof. Without a test, there is no testimony. Without belief faith wouldn't be proven. In 2016, I graduated from Ursuline College with my BA in Psychology. I have yet to reach all of my goals. However, I thank God for the experiences and life lessons. In each of them, I have journeyed on my other side of through.

www.ingramcontent.com/pod-product-compliance
Lightning Source LLC
LaVergne TN
LVHW010119170826
845678LV00012B/2493